D0828638

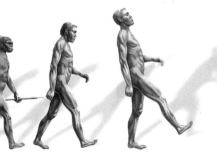

the
darwin Awards

FELONIOUS
FAILURES

WENDY NORTHCUTT,

creator of www.darwinawards.com

RUNNING PRESS

PHILADELPHIA · LONDON

A Running Press® Miniature Edition™
Copyright © Wendy Northcutt, 2005

Published by arrangement with Dutton, a member of Penguin Group (USA) Inc.
Darwin Awards is registered in the U.S. Patent and Trademark Office.
Additional stories and artwork published under permission of Wendy Northcutt.

Printed in China.

Library of Congress Control Number: 2005903357

ISBN-13: 978-0-7624-2562-4
ISBN-10: 0-7624-2562-8

This book may be ordered by mail from the publisher.
Please include $1.00 for postage and handling.
But try your bookstore first!

Running Press Book Publishers
125 South Twenty-second Street
Philadelphia, Pennsylvania 19103-4399

Log onto www.specialfavors.com to order Running Press®
Miniature Editions™ with your own custom-made covers!

Visit us on the web!
www.runningpress.com

★ *The Darwin Awards:*
Felonious Failures
contains cautionary tales of
misadventure. It is intended to
be viewed as a **safety manual**,
not a how-to guide. The stories
illustrate **evolution** working
through natural selection.
Those whose actions have **lethal**
personal consquences are
weeded out of the **gene pool**.
Your decisions can **kill** you, so
pay attention and **stay alive**.

*This book is
dedicated to
Malcolm McGookin,
the artist
whose fine work graces
these pages.*

CONTENTS

"I did not go to his funeral, but I wrote a nice note saying I approved of it."

—Mark Twain,
OFFICIAL PUNDIT TO THE DARWIN AWARDS

LAWBREAKERS and law enforcers bump elbows in an informal competition to see who's best suited to lose the FIGHT BETWEEN GOOD AND EVIL. Inept bunglers from both sides of the law, con artists to beat cops, JUDGES to CROOKS, astonish us with their casual disregard for the consequences of defying the LAWS—of Physics, and the RULES—of COMMON SENSE!

WHAT ARE THE
DARWIN AWARDS?

The Darwin Awards salute the improvement of the human race by honoring those who accidentally remove themselves from it in really stupid ways. Of necessity, this honor is generally bestowed posthumously.

Certain rules must be followed, to be eligible for a Darwin Award:

1. Reproduction
2. Excellence
3. Self-Selection
4. Maturity
5. Veracity

In other words, the recipient must remove himself (3) from the gene pool (1) with an astounding misapplication of judgment (2) that even a child could see (4) spelled trouble. And the event must be verified (5).

Four Categories of Stories Comprise the Awards:

›› DARWIN AWARDS nominees lost their reproductive capacity by killing or sterilizing themselves, and this is the only category eligible to win a Darwin Award.

›› HONORABLE MENTIONS are foolish misadventures that stop short of the ultimate sacrifice, but still illustrate the innovative spirit of Darwin Award candidates.

>> URBAN LEGENDS are cautionary tales of evolution in action. Various versions are widely circulated, but their origins are largely unknown. They are fables, and any resemblance to actual events, or to persons living or dead, is purely coincidental.

>> PERSONAL ACCOUNTS were submitted by loyal readers blowing the whistle on stupidity, and are plausible but usually unverified narratives. In some cases readers submitting Personal Accounts have been identi-

fied with their permission, but this does not necessarily mean that the sources are directly associated with their Personal Accounts.

Are the Darwin Awards Stories True?

Darwin Awards and Honorable Mentions are known or believed to be true. Look for the words *Confirmed by Darwin* under the title, which generally indicate that a story was backed up by multiple submissions and by more than one reputable media source.

Unconfirmed by Darwin indicates fewer credible submissions and the unavailability of direct confirmation of media sources. In "unconfirmed" Darwin Awards or Honorable Mentions, names have often been changed and details of events have been altered to protect the innocent (and for that matter, the guilty).

The Darwin Awards are "of the people, by the people, and for the people."
The website www.darwinawards.com
coordinates a worldwide community
of correspondents, who make sure
that egregious stupidity does not go
unnoted. Each story begins as an
implausible but (presumably) true
news report, and an alert reader who
culls the nomination from the media.

Submissions are scrutinized daily
by volunteer moderators, who select

the best for the Slush Pile. Readers vote on the merits of these submissions, and use the ranking to select stories that adhere to the rules and spirit of the Darwin Awards, and write them in a jocular vein. My sense of humor is refined by enthusiastic website readers, who vote, point out errors, add information, and dispute dubious details. During this polishing process, stories are often modified and occasionally removed from consideration. Thus the Darwin Awards in this book are not guaranteed to be accurate, and the most up-to-date information about each story can be found on the website.

The stories in *The Darwin Awards: Felonious Failures* focus on crime, as it manifests in the Darwinian process of natural selection among criminals. Living outside the law is a time-honored tradition, but an increasingly dangerous profession. In the lexicon of Charles Darwin's Awards, the perpetrators of the following errors are simply Accidents Waiting to Happen!

THE AWARDS

DARWIN AWARD:
MURDEROUS AFFAIR

Confirmed by Darwin

Regarding William Padgett. The first article sets the stage, the second details his innovative way of killing himself.

31 July 1878, England

William, better know as "Old Bill" Padgett, appeared before Justice Brown, charged with attempting to discharge a loaded gun with intent to kill Charles Marshman, for whom he worked upon a farm. The examination showed that on Thursday Bill became angered at Marshman and drew a rifle on him and pulled the trigger; but the cap failed to explode. Marshman struck Bill with a stick of wood, and his fists, and drove him off to the barn, where some parties took the gun away from him and he fled to the woods, where he was found by the officer. Bill is not a very handsome or pleasant looking man when he is all right, and the beating he received had not added to his personal charms. He looked as though he had tempted death by tickling the hind foot of a healthy mule. It was shown that Bill did not know the gun was loaded, he having set it away unloaded, and Marshman had loaded it unbeknown to him. He was held for assault and battery, and on Monday a trial by jury was held. The jury brought in a verdict of "not guilty."

1 February 1887

James and William Padgett were of

the first who commenced the settle-
ment of this town and voted at this
first election. They settled a few miles
from the village near a stream, which
has since been called after them. Bear
Trap Falls on this same stream came
by its name in the following way: A
few of their neighbors constructed
what is called a "deadfall" or primitive
bear trap, built in the form of a figure
four, with a heavy piece of timber
made sharp on one side to fall upon
and hold any large animal when
caught under it. This was in the

autumn of 1800. One morning William Padgett while alone examined the trap to see if it was adjusted correctly. It was, for the sharp log fell and imprisoned the unfortunate man, and several hours elapsed before anyone came to his release. He was taken out, called for a drink of water, which was brought him in a hat from the stream nearby, when he drank it and immediately expired.

Reference: *Oxford Times*, Reel 9, July 31, 1878, *Oxford Times*, Reel 11, February 1, 1887

HONORABLE MENTION:
ALL ABOARD

Unconfirmed by Darwin

17 September 2000, Australia

Six young men and women with no sailing experience were rescued from a stolen luxury yacht after drifting into a pier only four hundred meters from the boat's mooring.

They had intended to sail around the world, and had packed all the essentials: sixty cans of baked beans, one thousand condoms, some liquor and cola, and a library book on navigating by the stars. Luckily for them they were caught, as police report that "they had no fresh water and no food other than baked beans."

The would-be sailors have been charged with unlawful use of a vessel. We can all be glad that at least with a thousand condoms, they weren't planning to breed.

Reference: *Victoria Sunday Herald*

DARWIN AWARD:
HANGING AROUND JAIL

Confirmed by Darwin

2 April 1998, Wisconsin

Correctional institutions abound with "jailhouse lawyers" who will play any legal angle to improve their situations. Joseph, a twenty-year-old inmate of the Stevens Point Jail, planned a circuitous route to freedom. He would pretend to be crazy in order to be transferred to the minimum-security mental health facility, from which it would be easier to engineer an escape. What would a crazy person do if he were trapped in jail? Joseph pondered the question, then decided to hang himself with a bed sheet until he was unconscious, while his bunkmate alerted officials, who would cut him down and hopefully send him to the nuthouse. Joseph's escape plan worked more quickly than he had anticipated.

He hanged himself and was taken to the freedom of a grave the very next day.

Reference: *Louisville Eccentric Observer*

★ "Proof that God has a warped sense of humor."

HONORABLE MENTION:
PLANE STUPID

Unconfirmed by Darwin

5 February 1981, California

Phoenix Field airport had been subject to recurring petty thefts from neighborhood teenagers, so a security firm was retained to patrol the grounds. Thefts decreased sharply, but fuel consumption was on the rise. This puzzling situation continued until late one night, when a passerby noticed a flaming airplane on the field.

By the time the fire department arrived, the plane had completely melted into the tarmac. While they extinguished the residual flames, the passerby noticed a uniformed figure lying facedown several yards away. It was a security guard!

He was revived and questioned.

Turns out he had been siphoning fuel from small planes to use in his car. The plane he selected that night had a unique fuel storage system involving hollow, baffled wing spars. When the determined guard shoved the siphon in, it stubbed against the first baffle. No matter how he twisted, pushed, and pulled the hose, he could not siphon any fuel from the plane. Exasperated, he lit a match to see inside the tank . . . and the rest is history.

Reference: Submitted by David L. Baker, *Sacramento Bee*

"Of all the things I've lost, I miss my mind the most."

DARWIN AWARD:
STONED SLEEP

Confirmed by Darwin

26 March 2000, South Carolina

A North Carolina woman learned a hard lesson about drugs when she decided to sleep on the roof. Police reports say that Patricia and her boyfriend had been drinking and smoking marijuana, when they decided to enjoy the fresh air on the roof of the King Charles Inn. They

climbed over a guardrail with pillows and blankets, and fell asleep under the stars. Sound asleep, apparently. Patricia slid off the roof and fell to her death on Hasell Street shortly before dawn on Sunday. When police arrived at the scene, the boyfriend was found still sleeping on the roof, curled up in a blanket and pillow. The death has been ruled accidental, but we feel that the blame lies with the stoned woman who chose to snooze on the roof.

References: News and Observer Publishing Company, Associated Press

HONORABLE MENTION:
KLUTZY CROOK

Unconfirmed by Darwin

February 1998

ATMs have become a popular target for thieves. The law of averages demands that some attempts end unsuccessfully. Our hero knew that in order to collect the prize, he needed to get at the back of a money machine. He pried one away from the wall with difficulty. As soon as he had enough clearance, he wriggled behind it and started working on removing the rear panel. At this point, some problems with his strategy came into play. He completely ignored the video camera, and apparently did not realize that a silent alarm is triggered if an ATM machine is moved. Furthermore, the ATM in question happened to be only three minutes away from a police station.

As the sirens neared, our novice criminal decided to hide. When the police arrived, they saw only that the machine had been tampered with, and assumed that the perpetrator had fled the scene of the crime. They secured the area and called in a forensics team.

The forensics team was dusting for fingerprints when they heard a very loud sneeze from behind the ATM.

It was not difficult to apprehend the suspect, as he was videotaped, left fingerprints, and chose to hide behind the ATM.

Reference: Sean Barr, personal account, and VOCM Radio

DARWIN AWARD:
JUMPING JACK CASH

Unconfirmed by Darwin

March 2000, Arizona

The Grand Canyon is cordoned off by a fence around the more treacherous overlooks, to prevent unsteady sightseers from tottering to their deaths. Some of these overlooks have small towering plateaus a short distance from the fence. Tourists toss coins onto the plateaus like dry wishing

wells. Quite a few coins pile up on the surfaces, while others fall to the valley floor far below.

One entrepreneur climbed over the fence with a bag, and leapt to one of the precarious, coin-covered perches. He filled the bag with booty, then tried to leap back to the fence with the coins. But the heavy bag arrested his jump, and several tourists were treated to a view of his plunge to the bottom of the Grand Canyon. He did not survive to harvest the piles of coins that had suffered his same fate.

HONORABLE MENTION:
THE STING

Confirmed by **Darwin**

2001, California

"You won the lottery!"

California fugitives hoping to collect $1,500 in lottery winnings walked into a police sting aimed at serving outstanding felony warrants. The nonexistent Fresno County Lottery Commission sent thirty-two hundred letters, claiming to be distributing $78 million in excess lottery funds. The winners were instructed to present identification at the County Fairgrounds.

They arrived to find a balloon and streamer-festooned building, where they left their smiling relatives as one by one they were called into separate rooms to receive their surprise.

Uniformed officers were standing by to explain the hoax and arrest the befuddled fugitives. The operation served eighty-one felony warrants

and seventy-five **arrests**, and a
surveillance team **arres**ted two men
on suspicion of car **burg**lary.

Reference: *Fresno Bee* **an**d Mom

"Sperm: To be fastest
doesn't imply that
you are smartest."

DARWIN AWARD:
RESTAURANT THIEF

Unconfirmed by Darwin

1992, Tennessee

A restaurant in Nashville is well known throughout the music industry, not only for its great food, but also for its star-studded clientele. It is not uncommon for the sidewalk to be littered with long lines of customers waiting for breakfast and the chance to see a famous country star dining there. The man involved in this story may linger longer in our memories than the average country singer's career. It seems that one of the employees, noting how successful the place was, thought it would be a perfect place to heist. Early one morning he climbed on the roof and walked to the exhaust chute that hangs over the restaurant's large flat grill. Upon inspection the perpetrator realized that he couldn't negotiate the tight passage fully dressed. If only he hadn't eaten so many free breakfasts!

If only he were a few millimeters slimmer! He decided to reduce his bulk by disrobing, and he slid naked down the exhaust chute.

That was the last thing he ever did.

Imagine the surprise of the restaurant opening crew that morning! As they prepared for breakfast, they were horrified to see a pair of legs dangling just inches from the griddle. What happened to our erstwhile villain? It seems that the chute was so tight, there was no room for error. As he slid down the narrow vent, he slipped and caught his own arm under his chin, where he stuck. He died by suffocating himself.

Reference: WSMV TV

> "One gene short of a chromosome."

HONORABLE MENTION:
FERGUSON 2, THIEVES 0

Confirmed by Darwin

January 2001, England

Two men were taken to a Liverpool hospital after trying to burgle the house of pro soccer player Duncan Ferguson. The soccer player in question has earned the nicknames Duncan Disorderly and Drunken Ferguson for his aggressive behavior on and off the field. He once head-butted a policeman, and spent six months in jail for injuring an opponent. This six-foot-four kamikaze center forward is arguably the most violent player in British pro football, and not the best choice of victim. Police arrived quickly to rescue the miscreants from Duncan's wrath. Only one of the hapless burglars required hospitalization.

Reference: *Sentinal*, BBC Radio News, UK National Newspapers

DARWIN AWARD:
GUN SAFETY TRAINING

Confirmed by Darwin

28 February 2000, Texas

A Houston man earned a succinct lesson in gun safety when he played Russian roulette with a .45-caliber semiautomatic pistol. Rashaad, nineteen,
was visiting friends when he
announced his intention to play the
deadly game. He apparently did not
realize that a semiautomatic pistol,

unlike a revolver, automatically inserts a cartridge into the firing chamber when the gun is cocked. His chance of winning a round of Russian roulette was zero, as he quickly discovered.

Reference: *Houston Chronicle*

"One can(not) learn from a fatal error!"

HONORABLE MENTION:
THREE TIMES A LOSER

Confirmed by Darwin

31 March 2000, New Mexico

Edward had some trouble when he attempted to steal a utility trailer from the Home Depot store in Albuquerque. He drove in and hitched a trailer onto his Toyota pickup, then drove off quickly—only to crash on Griegos Road. He then returned to the home improvement store and hitched

up a second trailer and drove off—
only to have it come loose and crash
seventy-five yards away from the first
stolen trailer.

Deputy Sheriff Scott Baird noticed
the two trailers on the side of the road,
and stopped to investigate. Just then,
Detective Bill Webb said, Edward
"drives by with the third stolen trailer,
and the fender of the trailer clips the
deputy's patrol car." A twenty-five-
mile-an-hour chase ensued; the
leisurely pace was set by Edward, who
"probably knows that trailers at high

speeds don't stay on very well," Webb commented. The would-be thief was finally pulled to a stop, arrested by Albuquerque police officers, and charged with three counts of motor vehicle theft.

Three cheers for Edward! If all criminals had a modus operandi as feeble as his, the species would die out from an excess of convictions.

Reference: *Albuquerque Journal*

DARWIN AWARD:
YOU SAID A MOUTHFUL

Confirmed by Darwin

18 May 2001, Illinois

A Chicago woman took revenge into her own hands quite successfully when she bit off the testicles of her rapist during the attack. The twenty-one-year-old man should have known better than to accost a woman twice his age and ferocity. When he dropped his trousers and forced her

down, she seized her opportunity and severed his gonads, rendering him permanently sterile, to the satisfaction of all but the eunuch.

The woman walked to police headquarters a block away and turned the testicles over to police. Shortly thereafter a man with a matching injury appeared at the Michael Reese Medical Center. Police put two and two together and cordoned off the injured man's hospital room, while doctors attempted, unsuccessfully, to reattach the rapist's genitals.

A hospital spokesperson confirms that our Darwin Award winner is now sterile.

Reference: *Chicago Tribune*, Reuters

"Remember, half of the people you know are below average. Natural Selection is merely attempting to decrease that proportion."

HONORABLE MENTION:
MORSEL OF EVIDENCE

Confirmed by Darwin

16 May 2001, New Zealand

Cruising police spotted a longtime member of the Mongrel Mob sitting in a parked car in Hastings. The officers stopped and searched his vehicle, unearthing a plastic baggie presumed to be full of drugs.

While the thug was being questioned about the contents of the bag, he suddenly grabbed the drugs and began to scuffle with police. He was subdued with pepper spray and a restraining hold, and police began to search for the missing baggie. Their captive, meanwhile, had become strangely subdued. He was white as a sheet and no longer breathing.

Turns out he had swallowed the plastic bag, which the officers discovered during their resuscitation efforts stuck far down his throat. They extracted the baggie with the help of pliers from a pocket Leatherman, and the man was revived.

Saved from a Darwin Award despite himself, he was jailed on drug and assault charges along with thirteen other suspected gang members whose seized booty totaled $30,000 in drugs and stolen property.

Reference: *Dominion*

> "Just because you can doesn't mean you should."

DARWIN AWARD:
GOOD TRUMPS EVIL
AT CHURCH

Confirmed by Darwin

8 March 1999, Kenya

A middle-aged thief sat quietly through the Sunday service at All Saints Cathedral in Nairobi. But when the offering basket was passed, fellow worshipers were astonished to see him stashing handfuls of the money in his pockets. Realizing he had been spotted, the miscreant fled from the church and onto a busy highway, where a speeding bus killed him. The cause of death? An act of God. The moral? Don't annoy the Ruler of the Universe, or you just may wind up a Darwin Award.

"Stupid is as stupid does. Stupid is as stupid dies."

HONORABLE MENTION:
CALL GIRL

Confirmed by Darwin

25 April 2001, New York

"Why don't you come back and meet me here?" He thought she was calling to arrange a hot date, but he was wrong. The twenty-nine-year-old rapist had not only assaulted his victim, but had also stolen $70 and her cell phone after poking her in the neck with a pair of tweezers he took from her purse.

As soon as he left her apartment, she summoned help, and police encouraged her to assist in the capture of the rapist. Under their watchful eye, she called him on her own cell phone and courageously coaxed him back to her building.

The woman was an excellent actress. Her attacker arrived for his "date" an hour later with a forty-ounce bottle of Heineken in his hand and her panties and cell phone tucked in his pocket.

Police took the man, trailing a long criminal record, into custody.

His victim really did a number on him.

Reference: *New York Post*

"Just another ripple in the gene pool of life."

DARWIN AWARD:
WRONG TIME,
WRONG PLACE

Unconfirmed by Darwin

3 February 1990, Washington

A man tried to commit a robbery in Renton, Washington. It was probably his first attempt at armed robbery, as suggested by the fact that he had no previous record of violent crime, and by his terminally stupid choices:

1. The target was H & J Leather and Firearms. A gun shop.
2. The shop was full of customers—firearms customers—in a U.S. state where a substantial portion of the adult population is licensed to carry concealed handguns in public places.
3. To enter the shop, he had to step around a marked police patrol car parked at the front door.
4. An officer in uniform was standing next to the counter, having coffee before reporting to duty.

Upon seeing the officer, the would-be robber announced a holdup and fired a few wild shots. The officer and a clerk promptly returned fire, covered by several customers who also drew their guns, thereby removing the confused criminal from the gene pool. No one else was hurt.

"Behold the power of stupidity."

HONORABLE MENTION:
SIPHON!

Unconfirmed by Darwin

2000, Washington

When a man attempted to siphon gasoline from a motor home parked on a residential Seattle street, he got much more than he had bargained for. Police arrived at the scene to find a violently ill thief curled up retching next to a motor home, surrounded by spilled sewage. A police spokesman said that once he recovered, the man admitted to trying to steal gasoline from the parked vehicle, but he plugged his hose into the motor home's sewage tank by mistake. The owner of the vehicle declined to press charges, saying that it was the best laugh he'd ever had.

"God must love stupid people, he makes so many."

DARWIN AWARD:
BURNING DOWN
THE HOUSE

Confirmed by Darwin

19 November 2003,
Yorktown, New York

John Napolski wanted to keep his
house in a quiet cul-de-sac off Route
132 just east of the Taconic Parkway.
His estranged wife wanted to sell it.
Neither of them were living in it. So
John decided to solve the problem by

burning it down. He accidentally killed himself instead.

As police pieced it together, John had doused the house with gasoline, then realized he had forgotten to turn off the fire alarm. Apparently not wanting to alert neighbors that someone was in the vacant house by turning on a light, he flicked his lighter to see the alarm panel, igniting himself. He ran to a first-floor bathroom to try extinguishing the flames, realizing too late that the water had been shut off. By this time the fire had become an inferno. He died of smoke inhalation.

The fire destroyed the interior of the house, but burned itself out before damaging the exterior. Neighbors alerted the fire department the next morning after noticing blackened windows and the strong smell of smoke. Firemen found John's body inside the house, along with an empty 5-gallon gas can. His car keys and lighter were on the floor near the alarm panel.

Reference: *Journal News* (N Y), North County News

HONORABLE MENTION:
HOT PANTS

Confirmed by Darwin

30 July 2004, LaFayette, Georgia

A Walker County man's pants exploded while he was filling out forms for social services workers in front of his home.

Daniel Gabriel Doyle was hard at work in his laboratory when uninvited guests knocked on the front door. Because his work was rather secret, he poured two of the chemicals, red phosphorus and iodine, into an empty film canister and stuffed it in his pocket before going out to greet his visitors. Two social workers wanted him to fill out some forms, so Daniel, 39, walked with them out to their car, where he sat down in the back seat and began writing.

"He kept fiddling with his front right pants pocket," said Patrick Stanfield, commander of the Lookout Mountain Judicial Circuit Drug Task Force, according to the Walker County

Messenger. The film canister was probably feeling a little warm by this point as the red phosphorus and iodine mixed together in a chemical stew, but Daniel was happy to know that he outfoxed the social workers and avoided discovery of his secret project. The two chemicals are key ingredients in the making of methamphetamine. What he apparently did not know was that the now-boiling mixture of red phosphorus and iodine would soon reach 278 degrees Fahrenheit.

"All of a sudden, a loud bang happened, and fire shot from his pocket. It damaged the inside of the state vehicle and burned clothing on the case workers." Daniel suffered second- and third-degree burns to his testicles and leg. He was rushed to Erlanger Medical Center in Chattanooga, Tennessee, before being hauled off to jail. Sheriff's deputies raided the house and discovered his meth lab. He and a female friend were charged with manufacture and possession of illegal drugs.

"That was one for the books,"

Walker County sheriff's Maj. Hill Morrison told the Atlanta Journal-Constitution. "I've been in this business for more than 35 years, and that's a first."

Reference: *Atlanta Journal Constitution*, foxnews.com

DARWIN AWARD:
CLUMSY CANADIAN BURGLAR

Confirmed by Darwin

1997, June

A suspected burglar fell to his death from a twelfth-story balcony early yesterday after being surprised by the Calgary apartment's occupants. Residents of the suite are shaken from the incident, and baffled as to how the intruder managed to access their top-floor balcony.

The occupants, a husband and wife, were home at 12:30 A.M. when they heard a noise outside. "We were surprised, but not nearly as surprised as he was," said the husband, whose yell startled the intruder into falling while scrambling to flee. The body of the burglar was found on the ground floor patio directly below the balcony.

This unidentified "cat burglar" lost all nine lives when he failed to land safely on his feet.

Reference: *Calgary Sun*

HONORABLE MENTION:
BODACIOUS BUD

Unconfirmed by Darwin

2000, Indiana

A gardener had the good fortune to raise a healthy marijuana plant in his backyard. But then terror struck! He received a phone call from the authorities saying he was busted . . . but they would not press charges if he brought the bush into the station, roots and all.

So he sadly hacked down his eight-foot annual and carried it into the lobby of the sheriff's office, where startled officers took him into custody for suspected felony cultivation.

Turns out the phone call was a prank.

Reference: *Indiana Bedford Times-Mail*

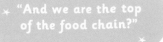

"And we are the top of the food chain?"

DARWIN AWARD:
TIRED OF IT ALL

Confirmed by Darwin

16 August 1999

Daniel was tired to death—literally—at the Buckeye Ford Dealership in London. He sneaked onto the lot in the wee hours of the morning with theft on his mind. His modus operandi was to jack up the back of a pickup truck, remove the wheels, heave them into the bed of a hot-wired Buckeye Ford pickup, and move on to the next target. Daniel possessed what local police referred to as "an extensive criminal background," and had apparently spent years honing his craft. But his expertise failed him this night. The pickup was half full when the forty-seven-year-old thief's next and final target slipped off the jack and landed squarely on his chest at 4:00 A.M.

A clear case of live by the truck, die by the truck.

Reference: *Columbus Dispatch*, Associated Press

HONORABLE MENTION:
WILE E. COYOTE

Confirmed by Darwin

1 August 1999, California

Myner, twenty-two, broke into a Los Angeles home at 3:00 A.M. on Sunday, only to be confronted by the homeowner, an armed police officer, who fired when he saw the glint of a weapon in the intruder's hand. Myner realized he was in trouble and attempted to flee the scene, but succeeded only in stumbling painfully into a bed of cactus, where he lost his knife. After freeing himself from the prickly plants, he headed toward the fence, a decorative wrought-iron barrier that speared him cruelly in the groin as he hurtled over to the sidewalk. Despite these blunders, he managed to escape, but was apprehended later that morning when he sought treatment for his injuries at the Anaheim Memorial Hospital. Sergeant Joe Vargas summed up his adventures by saying, "It wasn't a good night."

Reference: *USA Today, Contra Costa Times*

DARWIN AWARD:
ESCAPING CONVICTION

Confirmed by Darwin

December 1997, Pennsylvania

A prisoner in the new Allegheny County Jail in Pittsburgh attempted to evade his punishment by engineering an escape from his confinement. Jerome constructed a hundred-foot rope of bedsheets, broke through a supposedly shatter-proof cell window, and began to climb to freedom down his makeshift ladder.

It is not known whether his plan took into account the curiosity of drivers on the busy street and Liberty Bridge below. It certainly did not take into account the sharp edges of the glass, the worn nature of the bedsheet, or the great distance to the pavement. The bottom of the knotted bedsheet was eighty-six feet short of the ground. But our hero did not reach the end of his rope. The windowpane sliced through the weak cloth and dropped him to his untidy demise 150 feet below.

But wait, there's more!

Apparently the jailhouse rumor of the previous death did not reach a prisoner who was awaiting transfer to a federal penitentiary one year later. He tied eight bedsheets together and rappelled from his seventh-floor window, only to find that the rope fell twenty-five feet short of the ground. Luckier than Jerome, he merely fractured his ankle and scraped his face.

Reference: *Pittsburgh Post-Gazette*

HONORABLE MENTION:
DUMB DRUNK

Unconfirmed by Darwin

February 2001, Connecticut

A woman arrested on a drunken driving charge made an odd choice when calling for a ride home. Betty used her one phone call to contact Ken, her drinking companion prior to her arrest, who was visibly drunk when he staggered into police headquarters.

Ken failed a sobriety test. More surprisingly, a routine background check revealed that Betty had recently obtained a legal restraining order against him. A police sergeant explained, "We cannot allow him to come into contact with her—even if she says it's okay."

Ken was charged with violating a restraining order and driving while intoxicated. One question remains— was Betty or Ken the more foolish of the pair?

Reference: *Hartford Courant*

DARWIN AWARD:
GATE CRASHER

Unconfirmed by Darwin

Spring 2001

A wily car thief snuck into a rural estate with dreams of stealing a luxury sedan from its rich owners. He carefully opened the door without a sound and began to push the car down the steeply inclining drive, steering through the open door. He apparently forgot about the gatepost on the property. The door hit the gatepost before the wily thief could jump into the car. He was crushed between the door and the car's frame. A young doctor who had been told of "an unusual car-related injury" coming into his quiet rural hospital wondered why the man, who had not been killed immediately, never sounded the horn for help. The only help the doctor could offer was to nominate him for a Darwin Award.

HONORABLE MENTION:
PLANNING AHEAD

Unconfirmed by Darwin

February 2000, England

Warning to crooks: Don't expect the victim to cooperate with your plans! A bank robber presented a note at a cashier's window, threatening to hack into their computer system unless they handed over a large sum of money. When he returned later that day to collect his cash, police were standing by to nab him.

Reference: *London Metro*

"Darwin Awards: From Monkeys To Morons"

DARWIN AWARD:
HUMAN POPSICLE

2000 Darwin Award Runner-Up

Confirmed by Darwin

24 January 2000, Ohio

The Los Angeles Police Department contacted Ohio police hoping to locate a missing truck driver and his load of broccoli. The stalled truck was located in Ohio four days later and towed to a local mechanic. They thawed and refueled the truck and found that, apart from an empty gas tank, the vehicle had no mechanical problems, but the driver's personal effects and seven bricks of marijuana were discovered in the cab of the vehicle.

The trucking company and the police were both interested in the whereabouts of the errant driver, and a search was initiated. Shortly thereafter a patrolman noticed two feet protruding from between the pallets of broccoli—feet which belonged to the missing man.

The broccoli was unloaded as

quickly as possible in the cold Ohio winter, leaving the frozen body of the driver standing precisely upside down, attached to the floor of the trailer by his head. He was surrounded by space heaters and eventually pried off the floor, but his frigid corpse, arm extended, had to be turned on its side to maneuver it into a rescue squad vehicle.

The Cuyahoga County coroner's office determined that the man had been trying to retrieve a stash of cocaine from between the pallets of broccoli when he fell and knocked himself unconscious. He soon suffered a fatal case of hypothermia and died in the icy air. Perhaps this unfortunate soul should have confined his drug smuggling to the more clement climate of California.

Reference: Richfield Township, Ohio, Police Department Incident #00514

*Unconfirmed by Dar **win***

15 May 2001

In a poorly judged attem**pt** to con-
vince his wife he was sobe**r** enough to
drive, a twenty-nine-yea**r**-old man
pulled up to a State Police **barracks** in
his pickup truck, parked i**ll**egally, and
demanded a sobriety che**ck**. He failed
the Breathalyzer test an**d** was taken
into custody. "Basically," **an** amused

Sergeant Paul Slevinski explained, "his wife won the argument."

Reference: *Southampton Press*

> "Forget the adage about learning from your own mistakes. It's safer and more entertaining to learn from other people's mistakes!"

DARWIN AWARD:
SKI THEFT BACKFIRES

Confirmed by Darwin

February 1998, California

Darrell and his friends stole a foam pad from the legs of a Mammoth Mountain ski lift, piled onto it, and slid down a ski run at 3 A.M. on their makeshift sledge. The foam pad, lacking any steering or safety features, crashed into a lift tower which was—by amazing coincidence—the same tower from which it had been stolen.

Lacking the cushion of foam meant to protect errant skiers, the tower was an obstacle too hard for Darrell to overcome. There's a moral in there somewhere...

Reference: *Guardian, Sacramento Bee*

"A fool and his life are soon parted."

HONORABLE MENTION:
STUPID CRIMINAL TRICKS

Unconfirmed by Darwin

1999

These are random snippets collected from emails over the past decade. Their origins and veracity are unknown.

When two service station attendants in Ionia, Michigan, refused to hand over the cash to an intoxicated robber, the man threatened to call the police.

They still wouldn't give him the money, so the robber called the police—and was arrested.

* * *

Police in Wichita, Kansas, arrested a 22-year-old man at an airport hotel after he tried to pass two counterfeit $16 bills.

* * *

A guy wearing pantyhose on his face tried to rob a store in a mall. When the security came, he quickly grabbed a shopping bag and pretended to be shopping, forgetting that he was still wearing the pantyhose. He was captured, and his loot was returned to the store.

* * *

A man walked into a Louisiana Circle-K, put a $20 bill on the counter and asked for change. When the clerk opened the cash drawer, the man pulled a gun and asked for all the cash in the register, which the clerk promptly provided. The man took the

cash from the clerk and fled, leaving the $20 bill on the counter. The total amount of cash he got from the drawer was $15. Question: if someone points a gun at you and gives you money, is a crime committed?

✳   ✳

Police in Radnor, Pennsylvania, interrogated a suspect by placing a metal colander on his head and connecting it with wires to a photocopy machine. They placed the message "HE'S LYING" in the copier, and pressed the

copy button each time they thought the suspect wasn't telling the truth. Believing the "lie detector" was working, the suspect confessed to the police.

＊　＊　＊

A Los Angeles man who later said he was "tired of walking" stole a steamroller and led police on a 5mph chase, until an officer stepped aboard and brought the vehicle to a stop.

＊　＊　＊

AVweb, a weekly aviation newsletter,

reported that a bungling burglar broke into a Mooney aircraft at the Knox County, Ohio airport and removed its avionics system, including the Emergency Locating Transmitter or ELT. This device sends homing signals if the aircraft crashes. You can guess what happened next. The ham-handed crook jarred the ELT enough to activate it, and authorities had no trouble tracking the perpetrator to his lair.

*   ✱   *

DARWIN AWARD:
FAST FOOD FATALITY

Confirmed by Darwin

3 September 2000, Indiana

The felonious antics of two fast-food franchise managers ended tragically when their robbery cover-up scheme went up in smoke. Lisa, twenty-two-year-old night manager of a Burger King, conspired with a coworker to heist over $4,000 from the restaurant.

They staged an elaborate fake robbery/arson, in which Lisa acted the part of the victim bound with duct tape and trapped in the walk-in meat cooler, while her co-conspirator started a small fire and walked off with a duffel bag of cash. A key part of their plan was a quick "rescue" of Lisa by the local fire department.

Unfortunately the wastebasket fire went unnoticed until the morning shift arrived to find a slow-burning smolder that had never erupted into the desired blaze. The air from the open door caused the smolder to burst into flames, and firefighters were summoned. They found Lisa in the freezer, chilled and semi-conscious, and rushed her to a hospital where she died from hypothermia. Lisa's body showed no signs of forced restraint, the duct tape was loose, and she could have easily freed herself from her bindings and escaped from the unlocked refrigerator.

Reference: **thetimesonline.com**

HONORABLE MENTION:
AIRCRAFT AIRHEAD

Unconfirmed by Darwin

29 January 2001, Guyana

There's a time and a place for everything. But attacking your ex-lover with a knife while he is piloting a plane in midair is generally regarded as both the wrong time and the wrong place. Particularly by the other occupants of the aircraft. Karol Ann, twenty-one, was "suffering from a broken heart" when she stabbed her ex-lover and current pilot in the neck and shoulder. Fortunately for all concerned, a female passenger flying with her nine-year-old daughter wrested the knife from Jennifer's hand, and the wounded pilot managed to land the four-seat Cessna plane safely. Could she possibly have been unaware of the danger of attacking an aircraft pilot while in midair? Whether ignorant or suicidal, Karol Ann, who makes her living as "a star reporter," is advised to stick to writing headlines instead of making them.

DARWIN AWARD:
CRYSTAL DAZE

Confirmed by Darwin

2000, Mexico

Chihuahua, Mexico, is home to two hot caverns containing the largest natural crystals known to man. "Walking into either of these caves is like stepping into a sweltering, gigantic geode," described one awed observer. Some of the clear crystals of selenite are over twenty feet long.

The newly discovered caverns buried twelve hundred feet below the surface of the earth carry a curse for those who seek to plunder their riches. A man recently tried to steal one of the magnificent crystals from the roof, and might have succeeded if he hadn't stood directly beneath it while chopping it free. He was crushed by the sparkling stalactite as it heeded the call of gravity.

Reference: Discovery Channel News

HONORABLE MENTION:
ARMED AND DANGEROUS?

Confirmed by Darwin

20 March 2000, Germany

When the masked man stormed into the Volksbank in Niedersachsen and demanded money, the teller complied. Like a child demanding candy, the robber held his bag open with both hands and waited for the cash. Now, any fool knows you can't hold a heavy bag of money and a gun at the same time, so he put the weapon on the counter for a moment. The teller seized his chance and seized the gun, and suddenly the tables were turned. The confused robber raised his arm and, forgetting that his gun was gone, menaced the teller with his index finger. When the robber realized that his situation was not as strong as he had anticipated, he fled the bank on an old bike with pink protection sheet metal. The police are hunting for the man, but they have to take care. He is armed—with his forefinger.

Reference: *Bild am Sonntag*

DARWIN AWARD:
KILLING TIME

Unconfirmed by Darwin

2001, Scotland

Electric trains in Glasgow collect power from the overhead cable and transmit any excess through the rails to a solid copper cable that routes it to a power redistribution box.

Copper is a favorite target for thieves. One enterprising fellow with a good knowledge of the electrical system planned to cut the copper cable during the time between trains, when no electricity was traveling through it. His plan might have worked . . . but for one small flaw. In the pocket of his charred overcoat, police found an out-of-date rail timetable. The train arrived ten minutes before he thought it would, sending hundreds of volts of electricity through the thief's hacksaw and into his body, and putting an untimely end to his career.

HONORABLE MENTION:
LIMO AND LATTE BURGLAR

Confirmed by Darwin

1999, Washington

A penchant for life's little luxuries led to lousy luck for one bungling burglar. This Seattle bank robber rented a limousine, and instructed the chauffeur to drop him off at Bank of America and return when summoned by telephone.

The thief presented a teller with a

written demand for money, collected his cash and coins, and ran from the bank to a nearby Starbucks. While he was paying for a double latte with stolen silver, an alert customer phoned police and notified them of the criminal's whereabouts. While waiting for the latte, the bank burglar placed a call to his chauffeur from a pay phone, and arranged to be picked up outside Starbucks. The police quickly surrounded the store and apprehended the crook, after a brief foot chase, just before his getaway limo arrived. The driver confirmed that he had driven the man to Bank of America.

Reference: *Seattle Times*

"Another poster child for birth control."

DARWIN AWARD:
SCRAP METAL THIEVES

Confirmed by Darwin

31 July 1997

Two teens were disassembling an electric tower with wrenches when it toppled to the ground. They apparently wanted to sell its aluminum supports for scrap, but they failed to realize the essential role the aptly named "support" plays in a 160-foot tower. One of the men was crushed by the collapse of the ten-thousand-pound tower, while the other dug himself out from under, a sadder but wiser man from his close brush with a Darwin Award.

Reference: *The Associated Press*

> ✶ **"Darwin Awards:** ✶
> **Chlorinating the Gene Pool"**
> ✶

HONORABLE MENTION:
MIS-STEAK

Confirmed by Darwin

18 July 1999, Virginia

This steak lover will be a "prime" candidate for the Darwin Awards any day now. The story began with a yen for a good steak, and ended behind bars.

Cornelius became embroiled in a dispute with a waffle-house employee over the quality of their steak-and-waffle plate. Police were dispatched to the

Fredericksburg, Virginia, Waffle Hut in response to Cornelius's call to 911, crying, "They're taking my money!"

At 1:10 A.M. Sergeant John Barham arrived at the breakfast café and found the man pacing outside the restaurant. The man stated that his order of steak was not properly cooked, and that Waffle Hut had ripped him off by refusing to refund his money. The restaurant manager was interviewed, and agreed to refund the twenty-one dollars to Cornelius. The diner's victory was short lived. The sergeant ran an identity check, and found that Cornelius was wanted for a probation violation. He hauled him off to the Rappahannock Regional Jail, where he is currently held without bail pending extradition to Florida.

Moral of the story: Sometimes moral victories can be decidedly unsatisfying.

Reference: *Fredericksburg* (Virginia) *Free-Lance Star*

DARWIN AWARD:
COPPER CAPER

Confirmed by Darwin

1999, England

Wayne wanted to make a few bucks selling stolen scrap metal. He sneaked into a demolition site and surveyed the area for valuable hunks of debris. His eyes fastened upon what appeared to be a three-inch-thick copper pipe. That would fetch a fine fee! But it was too heavy for him to budge. He hauled a few lesser chunks of metal away, but could not get the thought of that copper pipe out of his mind. He returned with sturdy bolt cutters, and it was then, when he attempted to sever the pipe, that he was shocked to discover it was actually carrying eleven thousand volts of power. The paramedics who tried to revive the electrified Wayne were thwarted by the current. He did not survive to be charged with his crime.

Reference: *Derbyshire Times*

HONORABLE MENTION:
SPARE SOME CHANGE?

Unconfirmed by Darwin

1996, Rhode Island

Portsmouth police charged Garfield, twenty-five, with a string of vending-machine robberies in January. He was captured when he inexplicably fled from police when they spotted him loitering around a favorite vending machine target. Suspicions were confirmed when he tried to

post four hundred dollars' bail with four hundred dollars in coins.

"Out of billions of opportunities, these sperm were the best?"

DARWIN AWARD:
ROB YOUR NEIGHBOR

Confirmed by Darwin

25 April 1999, Australia

Darren was trying to break into a Craigie neighborhood house as safely and unobtrusively as possible when he wrapped his jacket around his arm and bashed in the window. But the jagged shards tore through the protective cloth and severed an artery in his arm. The thirty-two-year-old stumbled away from the house and through a park, and collapsed eight hundred meters away from the crime scene.

The homeowner returned from a nightclub early that morning to find a broken window, a bloody jacket, and a trail of blood. He searched the jacket and found that it belonged to an acquaintance who he recalled seeing at a tavern on Friday. He telephoned a friend, and they drove to the perpetrator's house to give him a stern reprimand.

When they arrived, they spotted him sleeping in the park nearby. As they approached him, they noted with alarm a trail of blood and his nearly severed arm, and realized that it was too late to lecture him. He had bled to death.

Next time try wrapping your arm in a bulletproof vest instead of flimsy fabric, Darren!

Reference: *West Australia Sunday Times*

HONORABLE MENTION: OFFICIAL DRUG TEST

Unconfirmed by Darwin

1997, Canada

A woman called the police with a complaint that she had been burned in a drug deal. She declared that a man had sold her a rock of crack cocaine, but when she brought it home, it "looked like baking powder." The police dispatched a narcotics agent to her house, who tested the rock and verified that, despite its appearance, it was indeed cocaine. The woman was promptly arrested for drug possession. The RCMP (Royal Canadian Mounted Police) are encouraging anyone who thinks they may have been fooled into buying fake drugs to come forward.

✳ **"Making the human race smarter, one idiot at a time."** ✳

DARWIN AWARD:
MODUS OPERANDI
MISFIRES

Unconfirmed by Darwin

1 March 1998, Pennsylvania

Roger, twenty-eight, was a considerate car thief. When the stolen cars became hot, he didn't just abandon them, he torched them. Setting the cars on fire, he reasoned, helped the owners collect insurance on their vehicles. This criminal habit became his downfall. A ten-year career of theft ended when Roger burned to death in Pittsburgh in a van that he had set afire from the inside. He didn't realize that the door handle on the driver's side was broken. His burned body was found inside the van.

"Better Dead than In-Bred"

HONORABLE MENTION: POOR SENSE OF DIRECTION

Unconfirmed by Darwin

3 December 1997, Connecticut

Maurice found himself in custody for making a dreadfully wrong turn, trapping himself in the lobby of a prison as he was fleeing authorities. The confused perp was leading police on a car chase from Suffield and Windsor Locks, when he abruptly pulled into the parking lot of the

MacDougall Correctional Institution, a high-security state prison located in Suffield. Maurice leapt from his car and sped into the front lobby where he was trapped by automatic doors that closed and locked behind him. Police say he apparently thought the building was a shopping mall.

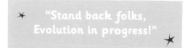

"Stand back folks, Evolution in progress!"

DARWIN AWARD:
SLAUGHTERHOUSE ROBBERY

Unconfirmed by Darwin

12 February 2003

Three men wielding knives tried to rob a slaughterhouse. But when it comes to hand to hand combat with sharp blades, butchers working in a slaughterhouse are more than a match for your average thief. They stabbed two of the intruders to death. The third man escaped from the angry butchers and fled in his car.

Police soon spotted him, and after a brief car chase, the would-be thief pulled over and leapt from his vehicle. But instead of fleeing into the underbrush, he tried to dodge heavy traffic and escape across the highway. Perhaps he thought that threatening butchers with knives was not a sufficient demonstration of his intelligence.

Within seconds, the natural justice system meted out his punishment in the form of a large truck, which struck and killed him.

HONORABLE MENTION:
PICK YOUR TARGET

Confirmed by Darwin

19 August 1999, Spain

A professional French pickpocket used astoundingly poor judgment when selecting his most recent victim at the Seville Airport. The thief, who specializes in international events that attract crowds of visitors, thought he was in his element when he circled a group of young men and chose his prey. Little did he realize that he was dipping into the bag of Larry Wade, champion 110-meter hurdler for the U.S. athletic team. He was also spotted by Maurice Green, the fastest sprinter on earth, capable of running 100 meters in 9.79 seconds. The two athletes quickly chased down the thief despite his generous head start. When apprehended, the pickpocket attempted to pretend that he was just an innocent French tourist, but the entire episode was captured on film by a Spanish

television crew that had been inter-
viewing Mr. Green at the time. "He
chose the wrong man," deadpanned
a spokesperson for the Civil Guard.

Reference: *The Times, The Times of
London*

"The line between genius
and stupidity is very fine."

DARWIN AWARD:
HUMAN TORCH

Confirmed by Darwin

23 November 2002, Norway

Neighbors called authorities to report hearing a loud pop followed by a fire at a rail yard in Filipstad, just outside Oslo. Fearing a potential terrorist attack, fire and police crews rushed to the scene. The top of an electric train, which was out of service, was burning. It took 20 minutes before the fire died down enough for its cause to be determined.

The spray cans and wet paint on the side of the train were the first clues. Clearly it was inner-city Norwegian youths, victims of a society polite to its core, lashing out in desperation at the brutal cleanliness and order of a country where the trains always run on time. So desperate were they to make their political point that they walked right past warning signs and climbed over fences to reach their objective.

One of them, a 17-year-old, wanted

to tag where no man had tagged before—on the roof of the train. The fact that few people would ever see his art was no impediment to this brave young man as he sought to subvert the dominant paradigm. He climbed atop the train, spray-painted his creation, and rose up to proclaim his accomplishment–touching the main power line and lighting up the neighborhood as 15,000 volts coursed through his body.

References: *Dagbladet, Aftenpost*

PERSONAL ACCOUNT:
GANGSTER BLUES

1999, Brazil

A car chase in São Paulo was so simi-
lar to a Warner Bros. cartoon death
that it had the bystanders laughing
out loud. A police car was pursuing a
car of gangsters, and both began to
fire at each other. Suddenly, one of the
gangsters had the bright idea to throw
a grenade at the police car. He pulled
the pin, cocked his arm, and in the

heat of the chase, he threw the pin out of the car instead of the grenade. The policemen saw the man doing this, and stopped shooting to watch. The hand grenade exploded in the gangster's car, killing him instantly and wounding the other bandits. The laughter of the citizens, the policemen, and the television anchormen was a paean to natural justice.

Reference: Anonymous personal account.

DARWIN AWARD:
JUNK FOOD JUNKIE

1994 Darwin Award Winner

Unconfirmed by Darwin

1994

The 1994 Darwin Award went to the fellow who was killed by a Coke machine, which toppled over on top of him as he was attempting to tip a free soda out of it.

Reference: Reuters, *Morgunbladid* of Iceland, *Kenya Times*

URBAN LEGEND:
CONTACT HIGH

December 2003, Australia

Glue-sniffer Bill Ball, 19, climbed through an open window late one night at the Durable Fit Glue Company, thinking he had entered nirvana. He made his way to the blending room, where he found not those measly little tubes of contact cement, but whole vats of it. Giant exhaust fans whirled to expel volatile fumes that, for some reason, the factory workers found undesirable. Perhaps they believed warnings that breathing the vapors could cause brain and organ damage—or death.

Bill shut off the fans and huffed happily, snorting in enough of the psychoactive ingredients to see "visions of Jesus, the devil, and a space alien," as he told police later. Bill had found his happy place. "I also seen the King of rock 'n' roll and ... it might have been Michael Jackson or that other singer, Kurt Cobain." He was so distracted by these visions that he spilled a 500-gallon vat of contact cement all over the floor.

The next morning, workers found him immobilized like a human fly stuck to a giant fly trap. According to a glue-viscosity tester, "We had to pry him off the concrete with shovels and a crowbar . . . and all the time he was squealing like a stuck pig, 'Don't hurt me! Oh God, just don't hurt me!' I told him to shut up or I'd super-glue his mouth shut."

Reference: *Weekly World News*

DARWIN AWARD:
ONCE BITTEN . . .

Confirmed by Darwin

23 January 2003, Winchester, VA

"He who barks last, barks best."

Raymond's new wife had often warned him not to play rough with her dog. But did Raymond listen? He did not.

Bailey was a wrinkly shar-pei, a medium-sized breed not known to be aggressive. Raymond, on the other hand, was not a model citizen. Not only had he choked his ex-girlfriend, head-butted her and given her black eyes, but the six-foot-two, 180-pound felon had just been released from prison after serving time for receiving stolen property. So when Raymond called his wife at work to say that Bailey had bitten him on the hand and he was going to kill that animal, she had every reason to fear for Bailey's life as she rushed home. But instead of finding a dead dog, she found a dead husband, lying in a pool of blood.

Raymond was said to be "a very intelligent man, but he didn't always use his intelligence in the right way."

Police concluded that Raymond had been beating Bailey on the head with the butt of a loaded rifle-shotgun, an alarming weapon with a .22-caliber rifle on top of a .410-gauge shotgun. As Raymond was in the midst of trying to beat the dog to death, the shotgun went off, blowing a hole in Raymond's abdomen.

Sadly, the dog was badly injured and had to be put to sleep, but at least

Bailey achieved a suitable vengeance against his tormentor.

Reference: *The Washington Post*

"Darwin's waiting room is never empty."

"The intelligence of the
planet is constant.
The more people,
the more idiots."

✳   ✳   ✳

"Everyone starts off with a bag
full of luck and an empty bag
of experience. The trick is to
fill the experience bag before
the luck bag is empty."

"Nothing is foolproof to
a sufficiently talented fool."

* * *

"Darwin Awards:
Retroactive Birth Control"

* * *

"Learn from the mistakes
of others. You won't live
long enough to make
them all yourself."

"Darwin Awards:
Natural Deselection"

* ✱ *

"Gravity:
More Than a Good Idea
—It's the Law!"

* ✱ *

"THE WORLD'S FULL
OF OXYGEN THIEVES."

* ✱ *

"Dumber than a bag of hammers."

"You can lead a man to knowledge, but you can't make him think!"

* * *

"One sandwich short of a picnic."

* * *

"I find it the greatest pity that she had thought to use contraceptive before her mother."

* * *

"Celibacy is not hereditary. STUPIDITY is."

"REINCARNATION:
Let's you keep trying
until you get it right!"

✳   ✳   ✳

"READY, FIRE, AIM!"

✳   ✳   ✳

"STOP GENE POLLUTION!"

✳   ✳   ✳

"And the Winner Is . . .
Eliminated!"

"Darwin Awards:
Culling the Herd"

＊　✴　＊

"Nothing is foolproof to
a sufficiently talented fool."

＊　✴　＊

"If teaching EVOLUTION
is OUTLAWED, only
OUTLAWS will EVOLVE."

"DARWIN AWARDS:
ADDING INSULT TO INJURY"

* * *

"Population Control Volunteers"

* * *

"Darwin Awards:
Tragic Proof of a Missing
'Why?' Chromosome"

"I DON'T THINK,
THEREFORE I AM NOT."

✳ ✳ ✳

"The Tree of Life is Self-Pruning"

✳ ✳ ✳

"Darwin Awards:
Natural Selection in Action"

✳ ✳ ✳

"Darwin Awards:
DIE and LEARN"

"DARWIN AWARDS: Where Evolution Hits the Pavement"

✶ ✶ ✶

"It's not the fall that kills you, it's the sudden deceleration."

✶ ✶ ✶

"DARWIN AWARDS: TOO STUPID TO LIVE"

"If at first you don't succeed . . .
then skydiving is not for you."

*　*　*

**"You do not need a
parachute to skydive."**

*　*　*

"YOU ONLY NEED
A PARACHUTE TO
SKYDIVE TWICE."

"DARWIN AWARDS:
Taking Care of Those Too Stupid
to Take Care of Themselves"

* * *

"Terminal Stupidity Is a
Self-Limiting Disease"

* * *

"NATURAL LAWS
HAVE NO PITY."

* * *

"DARWIN AWARDS:
Keeping a Date With Dense-ity."

"GOD'S H.R. DEPARTMENT."

✳ ✳ ✳

"The Extinction of Species."

✳ ✳ ✳

"EVOLUTION:
Nature's way of saying goodbye."

APPENDICES

Website Biography

The Darwin Awards archive began on a Stanford University webserver in 1994. Its cynical view of the human species made it a favorite speaker in classrooms and campus pubs around the world. News of the website spread by word of mouth, and nominations culled by avid followers flew in from far and wide. As the number of stories in the archive grew, so did its acclaim.

Eventually the Darwin Awards became the most popular of Stanford's biomedical research websites. It was encouraged to matriculate to its own webserver, and DarwinAwards. com was born.

The website is the locus for official Darwin Awards and associated tales of misadventure. Nominees are submitted daily to a public Slush Pile. Visitors can vote on stories, win Darwiniana, and share their opinions on the Philosophy Forum—a community of free thinkers who debate the merits of controversial nominees and enjoy philosophical, political, and scientific conversations.

> "Darwin Awards: The creative answer to the question, 'To be or not to be . . .'"

Author Biography

Wendy Northcutt studied molecular biology at UC Berkeley, then worked in a neuroscience research lab at Stanford University. She launched the Darwin Awards archive on a Stanford website, and emailed stories to a small list of friends. When academia began to pall, she joined a start-up company hoping to develop cancer and diabetes therapeutics, and continued to work on the Darwin Awards.

Eventually the lure of the Internet

proved too strong to resist, and Wendy abdicated her laboratory responsibilities to pursue a dream. She now works as a freelance webmaster, and hones her skills on the Darwin Awards website. Today, nominations from a worldwide network of fans are presented for vote and debate at www.Darwin Awards.com.

Wendy first learned of the concept of the Darwin Awards from her cousin Ian, a mildly eccentric philosopher who later started his own religion in order to avoid shaving his beard while working in the pizza industry. Ian is now pursuing a degree in archeology, and his hair is no longer an issue. Wendy devotes her free time to studying human behavior, writing Darwin Awards, reading, traveling, and gardening.

"Only two things are infinite—

the universe and human stupidity

and I'm not so sure

about the universe."

—Albert Einstein

The Darwin Awards Collection
by Wendy Northcutt

Plume Books
Penguin Group (USA)

This book has been bound
using handcraft methods and
Smyth-sewn to ensure durability.

The book cover and interior were
designed by Amanda Richmond.

Interior illustrations
by Malcolm McGookin.

The text was excerpted from *The Darwin
Awards: Evolution in Action, The Darwin
Awards: Unnatural Selection*, and from
the website, www.darwinawards.com.

Running Press Editor: Sarah O'Brien